THE
PLENITUDE
OF
EMPTINESS

hortensia anderson : collected haibun

DARLINGTON RICHARDS
South Africa and Ireland

nineteenth transfusion –
how much of the world
flows through my blood?

                          anderson 1981

Copyright © 2010

All rights reserved. No part of this book may be used or reproduced in any manner whatsoever without written permission except in the case of brief quotations embodied in critical articles and reviews.

Inquires should be addressed to
plenitude.of.emptiness@gmail.com

First printing: 2010
Edited by Moira Richards and Norman Darlington
Cover and book design by Norman Darlington
Cover photograph by Michael Rosenthal

ISBN 978-0-9869763-0-8

The Plenitude of Emptiness

CONTENTS

Foreword	7
Preface by an'ya	9
Introduction by Jim Kacian	11

HAIBUN

Letter to a Kidney Donor's Mother	17
Songs in the Key of Love	18
Sweetgrass	19
Ferncliff	20
A Passing Storm	21
Tracelessness	22
The Sickroom Window	23
Returning	24
North Shore	25
Farmhouse, 1825	26
Beach	27
Bayberries	28
La Chasse Aux Papillons	29
Fracas	30
Rahat Loukoum	31
Andalusian Gazpacho	32
Waves of Wind	33

The Lotus Pool	34
Ave Maria	35
Voleur de Roses	36
How Light Carves Shadows	37
Hammock	38
Mimosa Pour Moi	39
A South Asian Tale	40
Haibun with Zip	41
Strength	44
The Wait	45
La Haie Fleurie de Hameau	46
Verte Violette	47
Sa Majesté de Rose	48
Sixty Years' Passing	49
Passage d'Enfer	50
Kanji	51
The Spirit Clad	52
Blues in Black and White	53
Living Through Death	54
Next Door	55
Maybe You Can Come Home	56
The Comfort of Bubbles	57
En Passant	58
Riptide	59
The Empty Plate	60
L'Eau d'Hiver	61

Stroll	62
Water Stone, 1986	63
Nature	64
Claire	65
Impromptu	66
Half-Dream In Grey	67
Basho's Frog	68
Once Upon a Moonlit Heath	69
The Weight of the Moon	70
Blossoms	71
Leaving Pine Lane	72
If Waves Curled In A Row	73
Calligraphy Exhibition	74
Central Park Bandshell	75
Blue	76
Butterflies in Heaven	77
The Muse	78
Remains	79
A Dream For You	80
A Chinese Folding Screen	81
The Spell	82
Venus	83
Chrysalis	84
Syrinx	85
Recurrence	86
Burning the Bodhisattva	87

Amber	88
All The Way	89
Reaching Blue	90
Drawing	91
Diana	92
An Unexpected Chill	93
Mandala	94
Dreams	95
Turning	96
Ume	97
Nowhere	98
Calligraphy Exhibition II	99
Haiku Moment	100
Heart of the Pond	101
The Beach Scene	102
Gazelle	103
Calligraphy Exhibition III	104
Lys Mediterranée	105
The Gift	106
The Colour of Rain	107
Epistle	108
Platinum Print	109
Cameo	110
Chinese Checkers	111
The Way Back	112
Like Gulls Fly	113

A World Away	114
Blue Spring Oolong	116
Tea Bowl	117
The Light of Shadows Blooming	118
A Sunday Almost Night	119
Another Pier	120
Drift	121
Jazz	122
Density 21.5	123
Dreams of Wind	124
Held In The Stone	125
Remains of Myself	126
Lantern	127
Fleurissimo	128
Moon-Viewing Terrace	129
Childhood's Green World	130
Zen in Bloom	131
Tsukubai	132
Country Church with Rose Window	133
Wave	134
Acknowledgments	137

FOREWORD

Haibun is poetry that combines distilled, essentialised prose with haiku. First brought to prominence more than three hundred years ago by the Japanese poet Matsuo Bashō, haibun is a form of poetic expression still in its infancy in the west.

Hortensia Anderson captures the spirit of Japanese haibun with formidable accuracy, and her work effortlessly incorporates the Japanese aesthetics of *wabi* and *sabi*, as she delves frankly into her own personal experience.

It has been our privilege and pleasure to collaborate with Hortensia to bring together, in book form, the best of her haibun to date. The overwhelming tide of good wishes, assistance, and more offers of help than we could accept, bears testimony to the regard in which this brave and gifted woman, friend and inspiration to so many, is held.

Our thanks go to everyone who assisted and encouraged us in this very special project.

—Moira Richards, George, South Africa
—Norman Darlington, Bunclody, Ireland
March 2010

PREFACE

Hortensia!

… just her name commands respect, and even though she may have gone by others, to me and many poets and friends worldwide, she will always be 'our hortensia'. Most of us only know her 'online' but to make a long story short, I believe that anyone who has ever known our hortensia, knows that she is a fine woman and excellent poet to be greatly admired – now and forever after.

Hortensia Anderson writes and lives with her cat in the East Village of New York City and has authored numerous chapbooks and volumes of poetry over the years. At times, especially when critiquing poems, hortensia is a kind-hearted/hard-hearted dichotomy, however her many achievements in life and in writing, are grand enough that people listen intently whenever she speaks out.

Hortensia loves renga and other collaborative forms, plus experimental poetry of all kinds and is a virtual master at them. For those of us fortunate enough to have written with her, we are certainly all the better poets for it.

When invited to write a foreword for *The Plenitude of Emptiness*,
I queried some of her many friends and peers to see if they could
describe hortensia with only one word, what would it be?

Without naming names, here are but a few of their diversified
answers:

innovative
EXTRAORDINARY   Courageous
inspiring   vibrant   outspoken   superpoet
difficult   FUN   Mysterious   Teacher   Mentor
Unpredictable   Friend   WOW   seeker   soul-sister   Diamond
Self-actualized   Queen Hornet   inspirational   Unique
Chili-Pepper   awesome   Intelligent   Talented
Off-the-Wall   Zesty   Strong-willed
amazing

—an'ya, editor of *moonset*

INTRODUCTION

If haibun didn't exist, it's possible that Hortensia Anderson would have had to invent it.

Once in a while, if we're lucky, we stumble upon something that is exactly right for us, perhaps only for a moment, perhaps for a lifetime, but something that fits us so well as to seem custom-made. If we're not lucky, but creative and patient, perhaps we invent what we need. Hortensia has been lucky and creative: she came upon haibun at exactly the right time for her, and she has made it her own.

I don't know the circumstances that brought Hortensia to haibun. I do know that for the past several years it has been her vehicle of choice, and that she has written hundreds of them. When one practices so much it soon becomes second nature to think and dream in the form, and I believe she does, so effortlessly and copiously does the work flow from her pen. And the reward for her efforts is that she has become one of the best-known practitioners of the genre in the world, a regular contributor to *contemporary haibun online* (and its sister publication *contemporary haibun*), *Simply Haiku* and just about everywhere else where English-language haibun is published. In the tiny world of haibun, where everyone knows everyone else, she nevertheless holds a special place of honor.

Of course, the mere practice of the genre does not guarantee the interest of a reader. The work must connect with our lives in some fashion, enriching it, challenging it, broadening it, for us to accommodate a writer into our beings. And of course no writer will speak to every reader. But to judge from the feedback received at the *contemporary haibun* site, Hortensia has succeeded in striking a sympathetic chord with many. Several readers have indicated they especially look forward to her work, and seek it out first in any new issue.

And why is her work sought? I believe it is because of the humanness of her writing. Hortensia, perhaps because of her own precarious relationship with life at this point, is ever reminding us of our own connections with it. Her stories are fraught with things hanging on by a thread, the minute differences that spell success or disaster, a sense that not all is entirely within our power to control. There are many themes which recur in her haibun, but none, to me, more poignant than her effusions of childhood. Whenever she casts her mind back upon the past, what surfaces is replete with specific and telling images, often involving color and tactility. Fusing these images is a recollection of the specific emotion engendered, and not in a way that suggests an adult recalling the past, but rather a child still present—not a re-imagining, then, so much as a reliving.
I love the power of childhood she evokes, destroying the world with a casual sweep of the hand, as children do, and also recognizing her invulnerability so long as she is present in her pursuit. Her range in both dimensions—from childhood to adult sensibility, from the here and now to the vastnesses of eternity— usually in quite short compass creates a powerful knot of energy which, for me, shows no signs of coming undone.

There are other themes which she manages with equal felicity and panache, as you are about to discover if you don't already know. What strikes me consistently is the control with which she summons us to her reality—a few words, some well-defined space. Almost as if she had invented the form. Or would have.

—Jim Kacian, senior editor *contemporary haibun online*
Winchester, VA
5 March 2010

HAIBUN

Letter to a Kidney Donor's Mother

It was, no doubt, one of the worst nights of your life – the 10 pm rush to the hospital, a stranger holding your hands telling you of a car crash, a brain death, your child's name, a gentle request to have his organs. On December 8, 1992, at 2 am, your nine-year-old son's right kidney had been sewn into my abdomen.

I want you to know I named the kidney "Max", how I had a special pillow to protect him, how I endured such pain because I had been entrusted with a gift – and a sacred bond had been born between us. Yet finally, the following August, I felt a part of your son, a part you once carried also, die.

>   star-filled sky
>   our different wishes
>   become the same

Songs in the Key of Love

it had been over three years since i had been to our country house in New England. my aunt Leslie had been with us, before we knew about the lung cancer that would spread to her brain. as i drove along the winding road to pine lane, i could hear again her voice filled with anguish, "hortensia please, please tell me about death" and my refusal unlike the others, to lie. "i don't know. i only know that i have you in my heart always." "thank you" she said and lapsed into a coma that night, dying the next day. turning into our driveway, i caught the sun glinting off the two sets of windchimes we had both bought my mother. they were still hanging on the apple tree. although we hadn't known that the other was bringing them, we both chose windchimes with the same notes.

    sunlight through tears –
    small breezes carry songs
    through green leaves

Sweetgrass

She shows me how to weave blonde baskets with a light hand. As we braid the oval reeds with sweetgrass, their delicate but rich green runs through the wicker like rivulets after rain.

> darkness woven
>
> through the tangled leaves –
>
> summer evening

Ferncliff

As I stroll along the winding path that leads to the mausoleum, I feel a strange tranquillity – I haven't been to visit in years. It takes me awhile to find them – I keep getting lost in the labyrinth. Next to my aunt, around the corner from my father and grandfather, a smooth slice of marble waits for an engraver. I had begged for this niche until my bewildered mother finally relented. How strange, knowing the name and the date – except for the last two digits.

    columbarium…
    mourning doves
    a shade grayer

A Passing Storm

Before rain, leaves turn upside down and silvery as if presaging lightning. i pause in stillness…silence…the wait for thunder.

> windshift –
> tarnished clouds gather as one
> and break

Then, as quickly… trees drip greenness until slow enough to become droplets… in a golden calm – another quiet… one without waiting.

> after the storm –
> an origami crane
> floats on a stream

Tracelessness

Night and pain both have a love for the dark. Once again, I find myself swallowing another pill. I have lost count of the pale orbs but the pain knows, knows precisely. And, as a dreaminess flows in me, the pain ebbs.

"I should have been an archaeologist of myself" I say, giggling. My bones, bleached by the sun, will be awash, ashore. Hopefully, they will be scattered. No Voodoo nerves to pinprick this flesh and blood poppet or muscles to tie sailor's knots and angler's loops.

"Some day" I say, giddily. "They will wonder about my life over my death – yes, even though, oddly enough, the first made me yearn for the second." But, a snowflake has drifted onto my hand, melting with a sweetness that brings tears because already I am forgetting…

> my pale face
>
> in the dark window pane –
>
> a cameo

The Sickroom Window

Another night of rain passes into a day of stiffened joints. I force myself to get up to open the window. As I do, the world, having been held back by the closed glass, pours in. I let myself lie down again. Tightness loosens into drowsiness as a trace of sweetness carried on a breeze reaches me.

> gnarled peach tree –
> frothy blossoms
> cling to the clouds

Returning

My father was a fisherman. Before dawn, he surfcast off the coast of Montauk from a favourite boulder he liked to stand on. Ten years after his death, I return during a storm and come upon the boulder awash in waves. For some reason, I expected it to have gone with him.

    dusk in winter –
    a roiling sea
    churns the sand

North Shore

Our summer house was built in the 1920s and had a shower outside. During the day, the sun warmed the pipes. On hot nights, my sister and I took turns reaching up to tug the chain as the spray turned cool, then cold. I can recall her so clearly – shivering, almost blue in the shadows.

>washing our hair –
>streams of moonlight
>down her back

Farmhouse, 1825

The original gate has been blocked by hedges. Outside, moss covers the stone path. Light breezes carry wild mint through the bent cedar. Geranium petals splash their warm hues around a bird bath and through the green grass.

Inside, the red glass globe of a train station lamp, long retired, hangs from the ceiling. By the cold stone hearth, a broom with a short handle waits for a tiny witch. The smoke-grey cat, quieter now since losing his mate, sits in deepening shadow.

Awhile back, two sisters dropped by. They had been born here and wanted one last visit to their childhood home.

>   farmhouse –
> feeling the centuries
> in the wood

Beach

Held captive by the heat of the sun, we lie sprawled on an island of electric green towels. Overcoming my laziness, I reach into the cooler. The ice has not melted completely and the cherries are sweet and tangy, bursting with juice. We spit the pits in Gabriel's sand bucket and he carries it to the shoreline with a three-year-old's natural joy and tosses them into the sea. High above, gulls screech against the low rumble of waves as I feel myself drift into delicious sleep.

    a cherry tree
    from the ocean's depths –
    blossoms swept by tides

Bayberries

Climbing the bayberry cliff, Indian clay almost crumbles beneath my bare feet. Breathlessly, I hoist myself by clutching the sand dunes. Above the sea waves, I gather bayberries with my hands.

Boiling the berries, I let them cool until the wax hardens from dusk to dawn. Then, from dawn to dusk, I warm the wax until it softens. I pour it into wick-set molds.

> star-shaped –
> the scent of the beach
> in melted wax

La Chasse Aux Papillons

In my dream, I stroll beneath the lindens…the summer sun warms the orange and lemon blossoms, coaxing the release of their gentle fragrance to the stronger tuberose and jasmine blooming farther away. I awaken to the feel of a butterfly wing brushing against my cheek.

>unveiled –
>
>clouds part to reveal
>
>the winter moon

Fracas

First, faint neroli and peach among the greens…
then, the chaos of a million blooms unfolding…
white flowers, luminous as stars, tumble over
and over in dark woods of cedar and sandal…
settling at last, onto oakmoss in constellations.

> winter wind –
>
> a tuberose pegasus
>
> trembles

Rahat Loukoum

By the bank of the boat pond, Khadija and I lie down. The morning star has turned evening and the sun eases over the wisteria pergola.

Khadija sits up and rustles through her grandmother's wicker basket. On a gold-rimmed plate, cubed jellied jewels sparkle in a dust of finely crushed sugar.

I hold the tiny two-pronged wooden fork and pierce the confection. As I touch my tongue to it, a burst of simple sweetness is so pure, it draws me in.

Then, as I ease my teeth through the delicacy, the complex sweetness of creamy Noor dates unfolds around pale green pistachio and deepening Damask rose.

> Sugar moon –
> the prayer rug of grass
> hidden by blossoms

Andalusian Gazpacho

The tomatoes – seemingly ripened and reddened by the summer day – are cored and quartered. The holiest of trinities – fresh garlic ground by my mortar and pestle into paste, moistened stale breadcrusts and sherry vinegar from Sevilla have been stirred into a glass bowl – their flavours have seeped into brilliant colour. As night spreads her tablecloth of stars, I smooth the soup, anointing it with olive oil from Cordoba.

> almost autumn –
>
> a Flamenco tune
>
> on a lone guitar

Waves of Wind

Night-blooming jasmine surfs the waves of wind. With the full moon, its creamy blossoms open, their scent seeping through keyholes, silk sheets and dreams, lingering faintly well into the following day. With the sun, closed into narrow greenish tubes, the plant seems so innocent. But I know better.

    held in the flower –
    Majnun's love for Layla
    waits for a starry breeze

The Lotus Pool

Somehow, the air always seems gentle with stillness by the silent pool. With roots in the earthy mud, the lotus rises.

By dusk, blooms close, sinking through the dark surface of water. By dawn, they open again, to the golden fire of light.

But it is winter now; I crouch here, by the edge of fallen flowers. That flowing youth of a lotus in bloom has left, leaving her to a lonely, aging season.

>   a sheen of ice
>   on the lotus pond
>   leaves shrivel and sag

Ave Maria

A plaster Madonna – the feel of bleached bones. i dip the brush, stroke her outer garments and eyes cerulean blue.

For her inner garment and lips, an almost mauve pink… as if she had been left without a breath. i leave her flesh, her beckoning hands unpainted. at her feet, i paint blood red roses. then, i glue a piece of wood in her belly and hammer a nail in her womb, hang an oval mirror and place her facing west.

>centre of the sun –
>a golden halo
>surrounds your face

Voleur de Roses

After the thunderstorm, she hoists herself over the stone fence into the rose garden.

Petals quilt the rain-soaked grass. A lightning-swept wind blows through the brambles. The intrique clings to her like a secret mist. Before she escapes, she steals a plum – the ripe juice drips.

    remains of the thief –
    bergamot, roses, plum
    in the patchouly

How Light Carves Shadows

By pale dawn, from the west, she appears – a haloed silhouette. Then, golden sun reveals each chiselled fold released from the stone.

Dusk bathes her in oblique light, in streaks of rose, peach, violet, blue. As darkness falls, she rises with the silver moon, a shadow…

   the smoothness
   of her naked curves –
   light carves shadows

Hammock

Strung between two trees, the Mayan hammock is a light woven webbing of thin cotton strings. Together, cradled above the green lawn and below the blue-hued stars, the ecru hand-woven bed holds us from dusk until dawn. How I didn't know back then, the comfort of the fringe, twisted back and forth between my fingers, as I lay without you among the wildflowers.

    moonlight and shadow
    ebb and flow
    with the wind

Mimosa Pour Moi

Almost asleep, I slip into a world of green…a stroll along the rugged coast amidst the froth and foam of mimosa, whose tiny yellow flowers sing light and airy notes as they float off into the hyacinth and iris blues. Deeper into the dream, the sap-infused leaf and stem spray sweet cucumber nectar from branches swaying in the winds from the shore.

    across a dark sky –
    the moon trails pale
    chiffon clouds

A South Asian Tale

No-one knew it, but the sea had been crying. Around the Indian Ocean, the lace of her coral reefs had been ripped apart with dynamite. "for shipping" man said. On the coast-line, the lush mangroves with their verdant crowns, had been ripped apart by their roots. "for hotels" man said. The sea cried into the sand beds, into her mother-of-pearl shells she cried and cried salty tears.

On the day she rose, the wave had no face. Like an unexpected nightfall with the children playing in the sand.

>There they were once –
>children playing in the sand,
>swept out to sea

Haibun with Zip

i have a splitting headache. i can't hear well. i can't see well. since it's always serious with me, i only need worry about how serious. i put a message on my phone machine: "you've reached helen keller". friends laugh. i wonder if helen keller felt like she was walking through thick weeds like i do.

    in the tall grass

    knee-deep in shade

the only part that doesn't hurt is breathing. i have a phrase in my head: "the songbird's oval egg". i love the sound. in fact, i love it a bit too much. i wonder if i have taken my dose of paxil. then i wonder which is worse – if i have or if i haven't. another phrase: "waxy green mallard egg" god, how did this get into my head? fever? migraine? infection? all of the aforementioned? i can't decide if i feel too cold or too hot.

    beneath the snow –

    fallen flowers

my mother cringed as i told her i thought about dying just about every minute. for the last year. i thought very slowly "how did i ever live in you?" mother contains moth. flower contains flow.

a strong gust —

just as it blossoms

the flower flies off the tree

well, not really. i am breaking several rules of haibun here.
i might break another by jumping back to death. my god i just
had the feeling of leaping from a bridge and then magically the
reel rewinds and i arc in a fish-body-rainbow back to the bridge
landing on my feet.

painted koi

on a celadon bowl —

fish out of water!

let me try again. my friend mary eve is an embalmer. she likes me
to "talk shop" with her. she wants to run her own funeral parlour
complete with crematorium. i think we should call it "home on
the range". i've asked her if she will do the honours and embalm
me. once she called and said "you know. nobody knows what i
want. i might die first" and she might because mary eve is a very
heavy drinker. in fact, she drinks like a fish.

spring!
a vase of tiger lilies
wilting

(take it out! put it back! it's how you feel! so what it sucks! keep it in – it's not like it will kill you. alright, but only because i'm so scared and i want to distract myself by putting such a dreadful haiku in a haibun and keeping it there. is it working? a little bit actually! done now let's shift gears. should we put another haiku in? i'm too wiped out. OK.) i don't know if it is really spring yet. i can't tell because i can't decide if i feel too cold or too hot. i know i'm repeating myself. if i break all the rules, maybe i can leave a little shimmer of myself like Santoka. i feel so fucking lousy, i think i'll make it snow again even though the pear trees have just begun to blossom.

    the whiteness   of snowdrifts
    against my window the room darkens

Strength

Finally, I gather my remaining strength and make my way riverward. Foamy white waves meet the clouds. Windblown sails on the scattered day boats disappear, then reappear just as unexpectedly. Like strength. I collapse on a bench until the clouds blacken and shred against a gold sky. A hidden sun makes way for night. I can't remember a May with such a chill. I imagine it sharpening the points of stars.

>by my side
>the moon in the river
>wavers with me

The Wait

Such a wait since you left. I walk my reflection around the lake. The wind kicks up sending ripples across the glassy surface. A full moon shines down on her ever-changing face. "Just us two again" I say to her but she says nothing and a flowering branch eclipses us both.

    evening star –

    how will I wait until

    you turn morning?

La Haie Fleurie de Hameau

I have returned to the hamlet of my childhood. The tiny village is bordered by hedges of white flowers aglow in the moonlight – masses of honeysuckle drip nectar as jasmine sweetens the purple-black shadows cast by spikes of heady tuberose. The west wind remains in love with the hyacinth; the narcissus' by the reflecting pool remain in love with themselves.

    summer dream –

    the perfume atomiser

    shattered glass

Verte Violette

By my cedar with spicy-resin wood, I reach clusters of violets with fan-shaped flowers of subtle blue, heart-shaped leaves of tender green. I mingle the sweetness of raspberry, of rose with iris, a heliotrope resting with Emily Dickinson. I can recall it whilst asleep, dreaming, until awake…

    a patch of violets –
    the willow leans
    to touch their scent

Sa Majesté de Rose

Wind carries the scent of a woman in the Alsace region of France across the Atlantic. She is a rose held to the branch. Masses of verdant leaves spill dewdrops on silken petals. How one can forget she has thorns!

>summer fog –
>a green beer bottle
>rolls in with the waves

Sixty Years' Passing

On the loading ramp of a Berlin train station there are candles in the snow. The railway tracks at Auschwitz have parallel lines of flame.

In my early childhood, I knew old men and women with numbers on their forearms. Their numbers have dwindled. The German President was silent.

> winter fog –
>
> the stillness of barbed wire
>
> the absence of Japan

Passage d'Enfer

Trees twine like the arches of a cathedral. I have brought the three treasures – frankincense and myrrh melded by the warm gold of a falling sun. I step through a portal of branches, green mosses cool with the prints of a deer

...a light muskiness remaining.

There, a single perfect white lily is rising as if from a deep sleep.

    awakening...
    a strand of black pearls
    from a dream

Kanji

I dip the brush in black ink, make strokes across the blank white page. If you didn't know, you might have supposed it a Chinese calligraphy or in some other Oriental language.

The strokes are scars-sweeping half-moon curves, a tiny v flock of birds, vertical lines wavering upward, pagoda eaves, other horizons…in the language of my self, the kanji means "torso".

> scalpel –
> getting down
> to basic structures

The Spirit Clad

It has been said that in November, the veil between worlds turns gossamer. As I walk in the woods, a peculiar chill seeps into my marrow, kept warm by the spirits. I wear this during the month of transitions – of births, of deaths – in my family.

> North wind –
> a rusted scythe
> shreds the clouds

Blues in Black and White

Waves rise and reach for the stars but always fall. I have lost my voice to a dream I am unable to remember. The sky stays black despite the constellations. Along a crenellated edge, white-caps scribble their endless poem. What can they say that hasn't been said already?

> January wind –
> on a moonlit beach;
> I sink into my shadow

(in memory of Matthew Kasha)

Living Through Death

I fall asleep and dream of your absence only to awaken and rise to the surety of it. Your imprint on the sheets has been erased by my own tossing and turning.

The plenitude of emptiness overflows with pain.

But the last light of dusk is the loneliest, in a lovely lilac haze of clouds. My faith in the first star to wish upon has failed me. And the moon appears only if she must.

> winter sun
> a grey cloud covers it
> darkness at dawn

Next Door

On a dark and moonless night, white lilac drifts through an open window. It is the day after you died, the first I have to spend in bed without you. Next door, I listen to a man making love to his wife adding only my silence.

    stillness —
    six feet of ground
    between us

Maybe You Can Come Home

The black behind the mirror never alters – the scent of death permeates all the flowers.

"I shall take rememberings by dismemberings" the Commandante kindly said "and keep them for you" as he dragged my loves through white snow leaving a jagged red path like a ragged scarf in my memory.

> His ice blue eyes looked
> blood
> shot
> but his boots
> kept gleaming.

>> On a too distant cloud,
>> once
>> again,
>> the angel of history
>> folded her wings and wept.

> frozen moon
> we face the lighted ground
> a single file of shadow

The Comfort of Bubbles

Before I get to the beach, comes the grief. I have been expecting it like our child I once carried and lost. A sweeping stroke of sea and sand curves one into the other the way we once curved one into the other. It is your birthday. You have left me. Alone. Lonely. With only imagined memories of the night of your death.

A wave curls, its hollow mirrors the hollow in my heart.

As it dies, bubbles of seafoam at the shoreline join the sand with its bubbles of breathholes. Another wave has been born.

Afterwards, at the road, I turn back. There, amidst bubbles of breath and foam, I find the waves, waving.

> at ebb tide
> wavy lines of salt –
> aquarius

En Passant

All night it has rained and today, the sky takes on a delicate blueness. There is a freshness in the just-washed breeze. You wait for me by the gate to your loft – my pink ballet slippers soundless against the cobblestones. We embrace and I close my eyes, pressing my lips against your neck, the clean, distinct scent of you – cucumber and wheat. You open the gate to the scent of white lilacs in full bloom-lush, dripping petals reminding me of snow and clouds.

>   brushing my hair –
>   our shadows touch
>   in passing

Riptide

For hours and miles, I have been wandering on the beach. We were supposed to spend the summer here but you have died unexpectedly and now my life is adrift.

Between two stones I free a trapped blue-clawed crab –
I imagine she has gotten lost, trying to find her way.

    ocean waves –
    pebbles roll around
    in the riptide

The Empty Plate

The enamelled plums are plump and deeply blue on a creamy underglaze. Camellias bloom over the edges. Three centuries haven't wilted the pale pink petals nor dulled the porcelain's glossy finish.

    devoured…
    the clusters of ripe green grapes
    we held in our hands

L'Eau d'Hiver

In my sorrow, I try to capture the loss of you in a poem but the words and I – we keep missing. Then, unexpectedly, tears spill into a certain joy – I find the feeling in a perfume, like love itself.

It is light snow as it melts on my lips. It has the starkness of bare branches – darkly hidden yet there. Traces of frozen hawthorn and honey. Ice-glazed angelica. Frozen blue iris. A fragrance of mourning.

> l'Eau d'Hiver –
> another's dream
> becomes my own

Stroll

How lovely and sweet these climbers some consider weeds –
cream and yellow honeysuckle with their droplets of nectar; the
purple-blue fog of wisteria. I come home, petals of wildflowers
tangled in my hair.

    trumpet vine
    with its smooth coral neck
    a hummingbird hovers

Water Stone, 1986

Surrounded by a field of white rocks roughly the same size and shape, the black basalt tsukubai murmurs. It is like glass, polished smooth as the water flowing over its irregular edges. I wonder if, before his first chisel, Noguchi had already heard the sound.

> early Spring –
> as it strikes the stones,
> water finds its voice

Nature

As a child, I am told our blue-green orb has one moon. Across the alley, ten full moons glow in the windows. I call my best friend Sabine. "We don't have moons" she says. "Are you sure?" I ask. "Of course I am" she says. "We have eight suns."

>broken glass –
>we make another
>constellation

Claire

She never colours in the lines, this fragile child of eight. She doesn't even stay on the page, her blue crayon has gone over the edge and onto the kitchen tiles.

"We had such high hopes for all the girls," her mother, my friend, says "but then they told us about Claire …" It is a refrain, these words that serve as an apology or an explanation or rarely, a complaint about her "odd" child.

She is a patient woman, my friend, and I know how she worries about her third child, youngest and smallest of the triplets, the one she knows least yet in a way loves most.

Perhaps it is a blessing, having escaped the "high hopes" her sisters will have to shoulder. Of being forced to stop at the lines.

    clear blue sky –
    sunlight pools and flows
    into shadow

Impromptu

A lovely summer dusk…the sweet and sour of lime mojitos over ice with crushed wild mint. Naomi's cry "Let's do an impromptu!" convinces 20 of us to gather in a lower east side garden.

I perform a flute solo I composed at dawn called only "Impromptu". During the improvised coda, clouds gather, lightning flashes across a dark sky. Then roaring claps of thunder.

    shaking the droplets
    from the hydrangea
    a bird lifts off

Half-Dream In Grey

A light, silent drizzle. I float through the
pearly veil between awake and asleep.

A bell jar of mercury spills my reflection
and I cannot get myself back together.

Folded in silk sheets, finally, I find my
spheres coalesce into a mirrored lake.

I ripple adrift. Then, stillness.

> heavy fog –
> I disappear
> lost in thought

Basho's Frog

One evening, I have a raging fever. The next morning, I can barely hear. Testing reveals substantial hearing loss. I will need a hearing aid.

As I wait the week for the hearing aid, I sit by the pond at a friend's home, with a book of translations of Basho's famous frog haiku.

On the other side of the pond, there is a frog on a rock but he won't jump. I try to make him – I toss stones. I yell at him. I jump up and down. I splash my hands in the pond. But he just sits.

Annoyed, I return to the book. Suddenly the pages and my arms have droplets splashed on them. I look and the stone is empty.

>   green pond –
>   the frog jumps
>   into itself

Once Upon a Moonlit Heath

Remains of a day of aches – sharp lightning spikes of migraine, waves of nausea, thunder rolls heavily along the spine. A gingko tracing my body's path of pain...

    my heart   keeping sheep   by moonlight

Purple clouds dip into heather. A canvas of wildflowers glows through my window from another night across the Atlantic. Brushstrokes lift the darkness like a dear friend.

    pink violets   the softness   of her voice

(ekphrasis – originally haiga with title taken from a painting by the U.K. artist and poet, Sheila Windsor)

The Weight of the Moon

She stands nude on the deck, facing the Atlantic. Her belly, like the moon, is almost full. I have clicked through the last roll of film.

At thirty-nine weeks, she complains of feeling "like a weight", but her face glows.

The most precious picture I own has my mother, naked and kneeling in profile, not knowing my birth is mere hours away.

>first photograph –
>upside down
>inside

Blossoms

Flushed from their ballet lesson, they collapse across the canopy bed. "I want mine darker," Bronwen says wistfully. Her alabaster breasts have cherry blossom aureoles. "Don't be crazy," Gwyneth says reprovingly; "I want mine lighter." She lifts her camisole to reveal richly pigmented apricot blossoms. "Well, mine have to change or I will kill myself," Annaliese retorts. She is a pear, barely distinguishable except by texture.

In the next room, Charlotte (my best friend and Annaliese's mother) and I bite our lips to keep from bursting into laughter. "Should I?" I mouth to Charlotte. She nods back. I walk into the room with three lithe statues.

"Did you know," I say nonchalantly, "that there is a special rouge you can purchase for your nipples? This rouge stays put, through hours of lovemaking. Between the colour selection along with the flavours and scents, you and your lover can have whatever suits your fancy." As I leave the three blushing ballerinas, they whisper amongst themselves.

Finally, Annaliese musters the courage to ask, "Could you tell us of a boutique that would carry this?"

> in the mirror
> breasts full yet firm –
> I plié

Leaving Pine Lane

We had been packing since dawn. I had said my farewells to the rhododendron around the screened porch, with ballet slipper tinted petals that felt like tissue; to the ancient apple tree by the patio. It had never bloomed until the year we bought the house and I had caressed it and confided in it and loved it until it produced masses of blossoms and tiny sweet-tart apples.

>late spring –
>
>the sun shimmers on the lake
>
>through green leaves

But I hated the house without reason. I hated it the way I loved the grass, blade by blade – senselessly and passionately. We were finished with the packing up of the remains of our lives and of our ancestors. Dusk was beginning to fall deeply, goldenly. The piano was by the high window overlooking the lake. I touched the keys, lightly at first. Then I sat down.

>Chopin nocturne –
>
>the lower octaves warm
>
>from the sun

If Waves Curled In A Row

If I could dive sideways through an endless hollow, rocked to sleep in one sweeping curve, then waking to dream of breathing the ocean in a grotto of crushed pearl, don't you think I would?

   almost round –
   wave upon wave
   roll the moon's silver

Calligraphy Exhibition

A room of white square with black circles hangs on gallery walls. Bored, I escape for a breath of sky.

    enso —
    the emptiness of
    a full moon

Central Park Bandshell

The wisteria are in bloom behind the bandshell. We smoke grass as we have over the past three decades. A cop passes and I hold the joint out to him with a wink. He smiles and disappears. Beneath the trellis, we sit enjoying spring cool with the warmth of holding hands.

> blues concert
> through the tangled vines
> wisps of sky

Blue

I lead him to my art piece in the gallery – a pile of crumpled blue tissues. He stands, contemplative. "Origami" I prompt. "The Asian art of paper-folding to make things." "So with these origami you have?" he asks, delicately. "These are crumpled blue tissues" I say.

    Spring rain –
    a flock of birds
    loses their shape

Butterflies in Heaven

Before Sabine's mother dies, she calls her daughters to her bed. She is an artist and says she has decided to paint butterfly wings in heaven.

Afterwards, I tell Sabine about Kwan-Yin, the thousand-armed bodhisattva of mercy – it seems to me her mother will need those hands to hold the brushes.

    disappearing…
    a swarm of blue butterflies
    joins the sky

The Muse

This I can tell you with certainty – my muse has died. I discovered her swaying lightly in the closet, hanged. As I unknotted the noose, she sank into my hand and dissolved into sparkling ash which disappeared. All that remained was a closet with a silk rope.

She didn't bother to leave a note.

>Spring dream –
>a haibun in my journal
>called "The Muse"

Remains

The remains of the rose you gave me lie in dust in your love letters. How did it begin? With a single, perfect rose.

Had she been dead as I took her from you, the rose, helpless without thorns, her slim, green throat slashed on the diagonal – unable to whisper "stay away!"?

Clues in the letters abound: how your name loops around the page, how the "y" in "my" almost obliterates the "love" that follows.

So this is how it ends – with a faded promise of "forever", stained with the dark blood rust of a crumbled flower.

    betrayed by a breeze
    the light scent of roses
    hidden by shadow

A Dream For You

You feel a hand caressing you in a dream. At first, you think your dead lover has returned to rescue you from dreaming your life away. You awaken.

Stars fall through the sea, their light jewels the scales of tropical fish and play their lullaby in Phrygian mode. You float in and out of shadows on a bed of sand, as fine as crushed sedative powder, drifting, drifting…

You feel a hand caressing you in a dream. You reach out and the hand clasps around yours. You are asleep. I know. I dreamed you.

> tangled hair –
> lovers entwined
> on a beach

A Chinese Folding Screen

The wood bridge has a faded feel, muted by clumps of brilliant blue iris with gilded gold leaves. How amazing that all this loveliness has been flowing for centuries from one man's brush.

   splashes of ink –
   a narrow stream branches
   into eight channels

The Spell

Spirits in the wine escape the bottle and enchant us – body, mind and soul. Last night, we made love with the passion of the lovers we once were. Today, my heart overflows with an emptiness I have known too often and too well.

>wild grapes –
>ripeness bursts
>through the skins

Venus

Through the seafoam you found me, ground me into swirls of sand as the evening star turned morning.

I sit by the shore, lost in memory.

The sea reaches out to me in waves as I wonder if a single grain in the stretch of sand we made love on remains.

    venus —
    a pearl in the blue
    half-shell of heaven

Chrysalis

Aunt Hortensia! Aunt Hortensia!" Chloe calls as I sit on the park bench. She points at two butterflies threading through the lush green grass with their yellow wings.

"Did you know, butterflies were caterpillars?" she asks. "They change in a chrys – a chrys"

"A chrysalis" I say.

She pauses thoughtfully, then, "Imagine how they had to change."

I hold this child, remembering how I held her mother's rounded belly with both hands and felt that fragile flutter as if baby wings had sprouted in the womb.

"You are ever-changing," I tell her as she dances through the grass in the chrysalis of her imagination, singing.

    eyelashes
    against my cheek –
    butterfly kiss

Syrinx

According to Greek legend, the wood god Pan fell unrequitedly in love with the maiden nymph Syrinx. Because of her devotion to Artemis, goddess of the moon and the hunt, Syrinx escaped him by having the river nymphs turn the virgin into a marsh reed. In desolation, Pan fashioned a pipe from reeds on the riverbank, his consolation a melancholy song.

"Syrinx", the solo piece for flute by Claude Debussy, debuted in 1913 Paris. The original score is without barlines or breathmarks allowing for unprecedented variations in interpretation.

As I polish my flute to silvery light, I recall the myth, wondering if Pan waits in darkness for my first breath.

    moonlit night –
    a deer bounds into green
    forest shadows

Recurrence

You haunt my days because you live in my nights. I wonder if death rotted you away to parchment on bone. I knew nothing lasts forever. I didn't know only nothing lasts forever.

>buried
>in a second snowfall –
>blue crocus

Burning the Bodhisattva

Having chosen a piece of wood for reasons I cannot discern, he begins to carve. Then, he rubs sandpaper against the grain, polishing the sculpture to a silken finish.

At the beach, I collect stones by the sea and create a circle. I gather driftwood and as Venus sparks her chain reaction of stars, he unveils a bodhisattva on her side.

We sit as the warmth of the burning woman envelops us against a chill wind. At one point, her tranquil lips almost seem to smile.

How did he know she had been hidden in the wood, waiting to be freed in flames?

>golden sparks
>light the indigo sky –
>darkness shining

bodhisattva – one who delays nirvana until all sentient beings are saved

Amber

The sun melts across the bay, spreading a patina of copper. Wind rustles through the trees, carrying the last rays of light with the first shadows.

As ripples reflect the burnished sky, I want to hold this fleeting moment the way I hold a leafy fern that has been kept for millennia in amber.

> antique violin –
> a chunk of rosin
> beside the bow

All The Way

After we make love, I call him, say "take me to the beach" and without a word, he does. He drives me all the way to Montauk Point.

You say you want to know, before knowing you don't, why I keep coming back to you, going all the way, but never staying, always leaving with him.

I will tell you just this once – he never asks. We drink. The sea bubbles into the sand. He waits. He gives me that.

>summer night –
>the moon wavers
>in my whiskey

Reaching Blue

How do they do it, I wonder as I lie sprawled in my hammock? How do the birds reach the blue in the sky? How do they feel reaching blue?

I have jumped out of planes, been lifted by colossal waves whilst surfing, climbed dangerous cliffs, done triple flips in gymnastics but never reached blue.

Then it happens.

As I row across the pond, a blueness seeps into me and I keep saying "The sky is so blue, have you ever known a sky so blue?" as a camera keeps clicking like the trill of a bird.

The photograph in the gallery by my friend Gabriela, considered the best of the collection, is a black and white, extreme close-up of my face. The sticker below says: "hortensia: reaching blue".

>sky overhead –
>a cloud disappears
>out of the blue

Drawing

He draws my bath in a tub hidden by hedges. I step into attar of rose and a mirror of far sky.

He sits on his wood swivel chair; next to him, a rickety table with pastel pencils and papers. For an easel, he likes to draw in his lap.

Finally, he reveals his studies – nudes of me, adorned with rose. One by one, I feel them draw us closer.

   a slight breeze –
   rose petals cling
   to damp skin

Diana

In a grove of oak, the Roman goddess of the moon bathes in a sparkling spring.

With her final breath, she runs fleet-footed into the forests of another dream.

Do not mourn – she has not been lost. In sleep, waking from dream to dream, you will find her – in a moonbeam, in the light the stars stole shining between the branches of trees, in the limpid eyes of a wild deer as she waits for you to stroke her spotted pelt .

> in darkness…
> the moon always somewhere
> in the sky

An Unexpected Chill

The southwest sun sets into purple dusk. The San Gabriel mountains make a rippling black line. Breezes blow soft and fragrant with white flowers – gardenia, honeysuckle, jasmine. I am eighteen, doing cartwheels in the warm grass.

Suddenly, I fall. Hard. I can't rise or turn around but I catch the moon shining silver on the blade of a butcher knife…

The next day dawns as if nothing has happened. Handprints around my neck gradually fade, and with them, memories of that night. I don't know it yet, but the pain of the moon's cold betrayal as she failed to save me will deepen.

> October moon
> the rapist's broken rosary
> lying in the grass

Mandala

As a child, at dawn, I gather shards of glass, rinse them in the fountain and make my "circle."

Broken glass abounds in Central Park – cobalt Milk of Magnesia blue, beer bottles from honey to amber, shattered greens that once held wine.

"She might cut herself" strangers admonish my mother. But she knows I have worlds to make and not once do I injure myself.

At dusk, with a twig, I scatter the circle and destroy the world, knowing there will be others…

> Tibetan mandala –
> the sands of time blow through
> the sea of space

Dreams

How often I dream of you, Daddy, always on a beach, in a fog. I try to reach you across the rugged sand. You stand by a boulder, swing the fishing rod, surfcasting.

I catch the shimmer of a silver lure on the edge of consciousness. How I yearn to stay as the sun burns steadily through the fog of sleep until I wake.

   stars on the sea –

   I dive

   into the big dipper

Turning

Alone on the beach, I turn as a yellow butterfly lifts from a piece of driftwood, disappearing into the sand dunes.

How I yearn to feel the powdery flutter of a butterfly wing; to slip through wild mint with a fresh scent on my breath; to soar across the sea without a shadow.

    following me
    around street corners –
    the wind

Ume

A breeze blows through a flowering branch, carrying the sweetest perfume. I breathe deeply, unable to stop, unable to get enough. As one blossom drops by my hand and onto the paper, I wonder how it knows to let go.

    painting plum trees –

    the brush runs out of ink

    at the petals

Nowhere

In a rare state of clarity, it occurs to me that it has been over half a century for me to find the "here" and "now" in "nowhere".

>   lost in the green paths
>   of destinations
>   a maze

Calligraphy Exhibition II

With one stroke of a sweeping curve, the black river flows through untramelled white.

    enso —
    the circles unroll into
    ever straighter lines

Haiku Moment

I sit on the jetty, a marbled paper notebook and fountain pen with shimmering ink in my lap.

>haiku –
>through the everchanging
>clouds, clouds

Heart of the Pond

We wait between stones thrown at the moon mirrored on the pond. It shatters in circles of light, spreading to the edges, returning to the center as if nothing had happened.

> embankment –
> purple liatris spikes
> reach for the stars

The Beach Scene

They embrace until, almost entirely beneath the waves, she runs, lying across a stretch of sand.

He follows. Standing, then kneeling above, droplets of sea dripping, his mouth crushes into hers.

She tells him nobody ever kissed her the way he does. How I yearn to say those lines…

> rolling in sand –
> we make love with the moon
> in the sea

Gazelle

Frightened souls somehow find each other. As I stepped into the bar, I found you.

By daylight, the forest of darkness dissipated revealing us naked, in a clearing. Thus, I fled.

Tonight, you clutch me, say you are lost without me – forget the three decade chasm between us.

So I relent – between my breasts, you dream like a baby – having lost this fear that keeps me from telling you my real name.

> a swirl of leaves…
> the startled gazelle
> bounds away

Calligraphy Exhibition III

I wait as the Master waits. He inhales and with his brush of black sumi ink, he exhales the enso on cream-white parchment.

    zazen —
    inhale the belly enso
    exhale the world

Lys Mediterranée

She takes my hand, murmurs my name, then gives it back.

"Ah, memories" she sighs.

Almost two decades have passed since I clutched her chill hand...

The hill is steep, nearly a straight drop into shimmering sand, a turquoise sea. Green warmth of angelica root weaves through grass wild with lilies.

"If I jump will you love me?" she laughed.
"I already love you" I lied.

Wearing caftans, we eat tabouleh with bare hands.

> sun aslant
> a casablanca lily's
> oblique shadow

The Gift

Once a week, I visit her with a gift of citrus to dispel the mustiness of the nursing home. We sit in rocking chairs as she culls a trove of almost a century of memories.

As I pass the well-tended gardens on my way home, precious stories from her life slip into mine like shared dreams.

    withered roses –
    I stir fresh orange peel
    in the potpourri

The Colour of Rain

The early autumn that she moved next to me, some of the roots had taken hold on my side. Branches had given way through slats in the fence I built. Twisted shadows climbed above the arbours beyond…

This late spring, her lawn will be a lush green but mine will be hidden beneath dewy, snowlike, silken drifts. They will be the most delicate hues of dusk and dawn in sweet, damp clouds, the colour of rain.

    by moonlight,
    I cut a spray of plum
    from my neighbour's tree

Epistle

I fold the blank page, slide it into the envelope. Hot sealing wax cools with my stamp of an enso. I pass your house next to mine, slip it in the box with your other mail. It is enough for me to know it has reached you.

> rambling roses –
> blooming over the fence
> between us

Platinum Print

The nude woman kneels on a bed as if in prayer. Light through the northern window washes over her profile.

She cradles herself, barely able to clasp the slightly shadowed belly in the shape of a tear, full to overflowing.

    another summer –
    I keep on growing
    into my mother

Cameo

She died before I was born, having destroyed the last traces of herself – diaries, photographs, letters – in a fury of flames.

Only once did my grandfather speak of her – the woman that he betrayed. He pressed a cameo in my palm. "Your grandmother" he said after awhile, dismissing me by abruptly turning away.

I stroke the profile of a coral face with wavy hair streaming beyond her shoulders. How I long to know this stranger in silhouette.

>moonlight –
>I step into a shadow
>of myself

Chinese Checkers

"Do you know how to play Chinese Checkers?" great aunt Maude asks. "I love Chinese Checkers" I say. She smiles and a girl sparkles in her blue eyes.

I lay her prize antique board with the hexagonal star across a table. As we put the vintage glass marbles in their half-moon slots, she jumps.

"Oh," her voice wavers, "I lost a green one." "We'll borrow an aggie," I say. "Let me fetch your pills."

I return with her five o'clock tea and silk bed jacket, without the aggie. Yet somehow the lustrous orb found its way to the carved teak star.

"Do you know how to play Chinese Checkers?" great aunt Maude asks. "I love Chinese Checkers." I say. She smiles and the girl sparkles in her blue eyes.

>gathering flowers
>she tells me to remember
>the forget-me-nots

The Way Back

As I drift in the lush grass, a monarch butterfly alights by my side. Suppose, as my aunt had told me, the dark map of lines on orange wings really is the way back to my childhood?

>swingset –
>I try to flip
>over the sky

Like Gulls Fly

Silver stripers jump.

I run across the rugged, rocky beach like gulls fly.

My father waits on the other side. "Hurry, Hortensia," he calls, carrying his fishing pole and tackle.

I scan for the smooth stones, leaping from one to the next.

As I reach the stretch of sand, he grins. We wave, then he turns away from me, striding into the sea.

> dream riptide –
> the surfcasting boulder
> awash in foam...
> a silver hooked lure
> disappears with his smile

A World Away

He doesn't speak about it.

Sitting around driftwood flames, ocean waves, on a beach, not unlike a world away…

Haunted by ghosts, by a woman – the moon lighting more meaning between them than the few words they share.

Holding her in the rains, rains unable to cleanse themselves of their memories – the dark horror which has tied them together.

He will never forget.

Before packing, he paints a haiku in Vietnamese on a stone, putting it where she won't find it until after he is a world away:

    no amount of silk
    can conceal the heat…
    a woman's skin

Tuyet Mai – her name meaning "snow-white apricot blossom" – comforts him whenever blue skies overflow with the black clouds in his mind.

    home from the war
    in one piece –
    something missing

Blue Spring Oolong

The tea has travelled from the Fujian province of winding mountain streams with gentle breezes at 3000 feet. The leaves, slightly fermented, are shaped by hand with liquorice sugar into pebbles resembling unpolished lapis lazuli. As the oolong steeps, the deepening amber emits a delicate aroma, spreading a light, unexpected sweetness onto the tongue.

> Spring
> sky blue sky
> through the leaves

Tea Bowl

She hands me a bowl so light almost nothing exists between my lips and the frothy flavour. As I hold it between my palms, heat seeps through smooth glaze the colour of a cloud.

   potter's wheel –
   the essence of emptiness
   taking shape

The Light of Shadows Blooming

Although we have never met, I take the haiku book* you mailed me to bed. Through the night, I get to know you. The next day, I send you a part of myself:

>   shadows bloom
>   along ditch plains road
>   pale wildflowers

Shadows Bloom : Haiku by John W. Sexton, September 2004. Doghouse Books.

A Sunday Almost Night

Down by the jetty I sit as the sun dips into the distant ocean, crossing the nearly straight line between sea and sky.

It vanishes slowly, leaving rays of light in peach and rose, soaked up by cotton clouds.

As they pass above me, hastened by a cool wind, I head back home, the sand still warm beneath my bare feet.

    moonless night –
    the sky becomes
    day's shadow

Another Pier

How did I find myself the lost lone one in alone and lonely by the pier we used to so love beginning…

    each other's echoes
    finishing
    each other's echoes

Drift

Through the depths of a dream, I can feel your touch…rising, roused, we glide in a featherbed, half-awake, half-asleep.

> scented sheets –
> white lilac covered by
> the darkness of snow

Held by you, on some wading pond, I float and arc – letting myself fly as bow, arrow and target become one.

The archer hits the mark.

> rings through rings –
> the glow of a Romeo
> y Julieta

Jazz

He kisses me out of the blue moonlight into the smoky dark club until after awhile I feel us making music…

> sax player
> before the tonic accent
> a swig of gin

Density 21.5

It begins with the haunting call of a platinum flute, echoing through dark woods to a clearing of crystal. I am a figure skater, grace notes pirouette on a pond of frozen light.

The flight of intervallic leaps from note to note may seem linear. Yet the sequence of interlocking spaces spirals out beyond time. It ends with the unfolding of an ice petal arpeggio.

The metallic resonance created by French composer Edgar Varese in 1936 feels as breathtaking as a frost flower in bloom. Applause rings out and I bow, having returned to the world.

    halo
    around the moon
    vibrato wind

Dreams of Wind

A light dusk is falling. The bath has been drawn, wild mint floats in this secluded grass clearing, hidden by hedges.

I wake from sleep to the pain of pouring rain.

Half a century has passed since that June breath I took at the rising dawn.

I know I must give it back.

    wind dreams…
    the sides of my self
    I never knew

Held In The Stone

I stroll across the park as the sun dips into the pond, spreading a layer of gold leaf.

Held in the stone of a granite bench, the warmth of the sun remains – final traces of day.

>night coolness –
>the rustle of cobalt
>in a leafy sky

Remains of Myself

The slab of Botticino Classico has a pale blush.
It is almost golden, glowing in the early sun…
He lifts the sheet, revealing a reclining woman.
I stroke the stone folds of my nude self.
Later, in the studio, I find a dark burlap sack.
Leftover marble chips have been swept into it.
It is as if I have come upon lost remains of myself –
how I yearn to keep them.

    rose moon –

    light caresses

    the curved darkness

Lantern

The apricot light of a lantern sways back and forth as a silhouette floats through shoji walls.

The nun pauses at the open door, her shaved head a shining moon. Gently, she slides the door closed.

I curl into my futon. Holding the lantern, she shuffles through the zendo halls into the night.

> on a breeze –
> the firefly returns
> to darkness

Fleurissimo

In celebration of the vernal nuptials to American actress Grace Kelly, Prince Rainier of Monaco commissioned the creation of a parfum.

The alchemists at the House of Creed (for surely the transmutation of existence into essence surpasses mere parfumerie) were to capture a woman's life in a droplet.

Upon completion, the elixir, a seemingly simple bouquet of four flowers, had the complexity of an ethereal other, paradoxically herself – her personal fragrance until death.

I spray my pillow and a fairy tale garden blooms with Bulgarian roses, violets, tuberoses, Florentine irises, but the lovely sillage carries me into troubled dreams.

> as the car
> misses the curved road…
> tumbling flowers

Moon-Viewing Terrace

A young girl, I peer through the lattice window onto the moon-viewing terrace.

Streams flow over the stillness of rocks.

With no moon, I hear a hushed cry, then, murmurs as soft as water surrounded by silence.

    light breeze –
    a peony drifts
    through darkness

Childhood's Green World

Barefoot, I cartwheel through clover as sunlight filters through ferns casting lacy shadows. At the pond's edge, I gather froth with both hands. How I love the bubbles, the way they reflect the leafy trees, cool in the summer heat.

> green frogs –
> the mossy stones
> "ribbit"

Zen in Bloom

    stone waterfall –
    a rock mountain rises
    from a sea of sand

Beyond the window, a monk rakes.

Tsukubai

By dusk, the sodalite he bought as a dusty slab of stone from the quarry at dawn has been carved by his sculptor's hand into a half-circle of royal blue sky with streaks of cirrus.

Gently, he places it in the grass. The garden hose gurgles.

> dipping my finger
> in the stone basin,
> i trace the moon…

Country Church with Rose Window

Breathless on the path, she holds onto the gate around the church. The statue of the Madonna beckons her. Aching, she makes it from the back to a front pew to rest awhile.

There, in the midst of pain, she feels the glow of glass petals – their hues fall gently through the window of Our Lady of the Rosary. Released, her last breath rises at one with the roses.

   climbing the trellis
   the sweetness of attar
   reaches the sky

Wave

"I want to be a wave" I had said, pierced by the pain of adult laughter.

How the ache of ridicule remains. I sit on the jetty as naked as the hurt child I had been.

Hot, salty tears stream on my face, cooled by the spray off the Atlantic.

    turning
    over and over –
    I wave

ACKNOWLEDGMENTS

Contemporary Haibun Online

Amber
Basho's Frog
Blossoms
Blue
Burning the Bodhisattva
Butterflies in Heaven
Cameo
Central Park Bandshell
Chrysalis
Claire
Density 21.5
Drawing
Dreams
En Passant
Fleurissimo
Haibun with Zip
Lantern
Leaving Pine Lane
Mandala
Maybe You Can Come Home
Nature
North Shore
Platinum Print
Remains of Myself
Syrinx
Tea Bowl
The Gift
The Way Back
Ume

Modern Haibun & Tanka Prose

A World Away
Dreams of Wind Winter
Like Gulls Fly Summer
The Light of Shadows Blooming

Simply Haiku

An Unexpected Chill
Chinese Checkers
Epistle
Ferncliff
Letter to a Kidney Donor's Mother
Remains
The Weight of the Moon
Turning

www.ingramcontent.com/pod-product-compliance
Lightning Source LLC
Chambersburg PA
CBHW071700040426
42446CB00011B/1850